POCKET Edition 100 ᴍᴀᴄᴛᴇ

Butterflies & Moths

Pocket Edition

100 FACTS

Butterflies & Moths

Steve Parker

Consultant: Barbara Taylor

MILES KELLY

First published in 2016 by Miles Kelly Publishing Ltd
Harding's Barn, Bardfield End Green, Thaxted, Essex, CM6 3PX, UK

This edition published 2019

2 4 6 8 10 9 7 5 3 1

Publishing Director Belinda Gallagher
Creative Director Jo Cowan
Editorial Director Rosie Neave
Editor Amy Johnson
Cover Designer Rob Hale
Designers Andrea Slane, Simon Lee
Image Manager Liberty Newton
Indexer Jane Parker
Production Elizabeth Collins, Caroline Kelly
Reprographics Stephan Davis, Callum Ratcliffe-Bingham
Assets Lorraine King

Butterfly Conservation

Saving butterflies, moths and our environment

Butterfly Conservation is the UK charity dedicated to saving butterflies and moths. These insects are key indicators of the health of our environment. They connect us to nature and contribute to our wellbeing. With the help of our supporters Butterfly Conservation improves landscapes for butterflies and moths, creating a better environment for us all.

ISBN 978-1-78617-654-7

Printed in China

British Library Cataloguing-in-Publication Data
A catalogue record for this book is available from the British Library

ACKNOWLEDGEMENTS
The publishers would like to thank the following artists who have contributed to this book:
Peter Bull, Chris Jevons (The Bright Agency)
All other artwork from the Miles Kelly Artwork Bank

The publishers would like to thank the following sources for the use of their photographs:
Key: t = top, b = bottom, l = left, r = right, c = centre, m = main, bg = background, rt = repeated throughout
Cover: (front) sunipix55/Shutterstock.com, (back) (cl) ilikestudio/Shutterstock.com, (cr) Sergiy Palamarchuk/Shutterstock.com
Alamy 39 The Natural History Museum; 44(l) The Natural History Museum; 45(cl) Robert Rosenblum; 47(tr) ZUMA Press, Inc
Corbis 24(b) Frans Hodzelmans/NIS/Minden Pictures; 25(c) Visuals Unlimited; 28(bl) Stephen Dalton/Minden Pictures; 34(l) Frans Lanting;
41(tl) Frank Krahmer/Masterfile **Dreamstime** 20(c) Gordzam; 22(bl) Sakda Nokkaew; 30(bl) Hakoar **FLPA** 9(c) Thomas Marent/Minden
Pictures; 10(tl) Konrad Wothe/Minden Pictures; 11(tl) Michael Durham/Minden Pictures; 18(m) Arik Siegel/Nature in Stock; 19(b) Michael
& Patricia Fogden/Minden Pictures; 21(b) Silvia Reiche/Minden Pictures; 27(b) Imagebroker, Adam Seward/Imagebroker; 35(bg) Ingo
Arndt/Minden Pictures; 40(tr) Piotr Naskrecki/Minden Pictures; 42(bl) Matt Cole **Fotolia** 8–9(t, rt) deardone; 34(tr, bg) Alexey Khromushin
iStockphoto.com 10(tr) KirsanovV; 29(br) Diana Meister; 36(cl) CatherineSim; 43(tl) Tree4Two **National Geographic Creative** 26(b) Darlyne
A. Murawski; 41(bl) Cary Wolinsky **Nature Picture Library** 7 Paul Harcourt Davies; 17(tr) ARCO; 36(b) Paul Hobson; 43(cr) Paul Harcourt
Davies; 46 Shibai Xiao; 47(b) Adrian Davies **Rex Features** 33(tr) Finlayson/Newspix **Science Photo Library** 13(br) Susumu Nishinaga;
14–15(b) Cordelia Molloy **Shutterstock.com** 6 aabeele; 8(panel – Riodinidae) Bildagentur Zoonar GmbH; 9(panel – Noctuoidea) alslutsky,
(panel – Pyraloidea) Pan Xunbin, (tr) Andreas Weitzmann; 10–11(card bgs) and 13(cr) non15; 10(tc) Matthijs Wetterauw, (bl) Frank
Hoekzema, (bc) AleksandarMilutinovic, (br) Matee Nuserm; 11(tc) Kirsanov Valeriy Vladimirovich, (bc) bigfatcat, (cr) neil hardwick;
12(quiz panel, rt) mycteria; 13(tr, rt) Kanate; 15(IDBI panel, rt) long8614, (m) P. Chinnapong; 17(m) iladm, (cl) Mrs_ya, (br) nuttakit;
20–21(t) jps, (bgs) Lucy Baldwin; 20(b) Krzysztof Slusarczyk; 21(t) and (c) jps; 22(tr) Mathisa; 23(cr) Hugh Lansdown, (bl) neil hardwick;
24(tr) Tyler Fox; 25(bl) Rob Hainer; 26(tr) M. Shcherbyna; 27(tl) Matee Nuserm, (activity panel frame, rt) Tim Burrett,
(activity panel green bg, rt) donatas1205, (activity panel bg, rt) Yummyphotos, (bc panel, rt) sharpner; 28–29(m) twospeeds;
28(bl) tobkatrina; 29(tl) Tyler Fox, (tr) Matee Nuserm; 30–31(t) Melinda Fawver; 30(bc) Klaus Kaulitzki, (br) Paul van den Berg; 31(tl) Sari
ONeal, (tr) Steve Brigman, (c) artpritsadee; 32–33(m) Cathy Keifer; 34(t, bg) Picsfive, (br) ChameleonsEye; 35(t) StevenRussellSmithPhotos,
(t, bg) Africa Studio, (cl) KPG_Payless; 36–37(c) guentermanaus; 38(cr) Matee Nuserm, (bl) S_Photo; 40(map, t) hagit berkovich,
(map, c) Dennis van de Water, (map, b) Ammit Jack; 41(map, l) Andreas Weitzmann, (map, r) Ivan Hor; 42(map) Randimal;
43(map, tl) A.S.Floro, (map, cl) aaltair, (map, cr) Bildagentur Zoonar GmbH, (map, b) Matee Nuserm; 44–45(bg) s_oleg, (labels) kikka8869;
44(l, bg) colors, (bl) Morphart Creation; 45(tl) grintan, (t, bg) nuttakit, (r) My Good Images, (bc) Evoken, (b, bg) BrAt82
Superstock 20(t) imageBROKER/imageBROKER

All other photographs are from:
digitalSTOCK, digitalvision, John Foxx, PhotoAlto, PhotoDisc, PhotoEssentials, PhotoPro, Stockbyte

Every effort has been made to acknowledge the source and copyright holder of each picture.
Miles Kelly Publishing apologizes for any unintentional errors or omissions.

Made with paper from a sustainable forest

www.mileskelly.net

The publishers would like to thank Butterfly Conservation for their help in compiling this book.

Contents

Fragile beauties

1 In the natural world, at almost any moment, a winged creature might silently flutter by. This is a glimpse of the fascinating insect group called butterflies and moths. There are thousands of different kinds, and they range in size from smaller than this 'o', to bigger than this page. They are vital to the places in which they live (habitats) – yet many are under threat from human activity.

◄ The name of the silver-washed fritillary butterfly comes from the silvery sheen under its wings.

▶ Many moths are dull grey or brown in colour, but the crimson speckled moth has vivid markings.

Scale wings

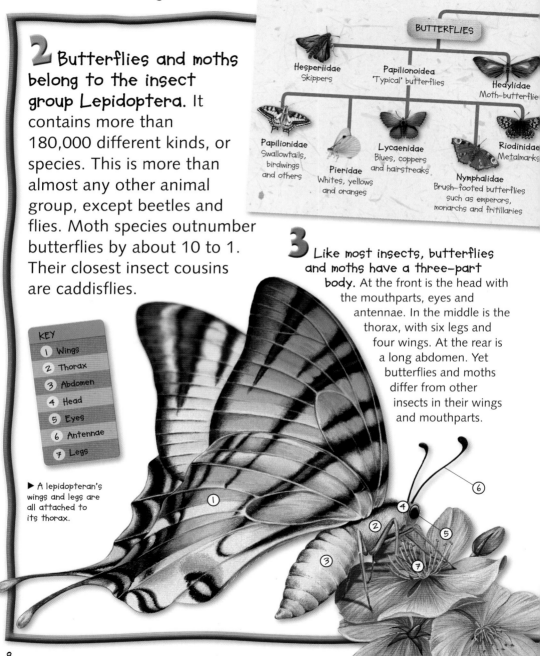

2 **Butterflies and moths belong to the insect group Lepidoptera.** It contains more than 180,000 different kinds, or species. This is more than almost any other animal group, except beetles and flies. Moth species outnumber butterflies by about 10 to 1. Their closest insect cousins are caddisflies.

BUTTERFLIES

Hesperiidae
Skippers

Papilionoidea
'Typical' butterflies

Hedylidae
Moth-butterflie

Papilionidae
Swallowtails,
birdwings
and others

Pieridae
Whites, yellows
and oranges

Lycaenidae
Blues, coppers
and hairstreaks

Nymphalidae
Brush-footed butterflies
such as emperors,
monarchs and fritillaries

Riodinidae
Metalmarks

3 **Like most insects, butterflies and moths have a three-part body.** At the front is the head with the mouthparts, eyes and antennae. In the middle is the thorax, with six legs and four wings. At the rear is a long abdomen. Yet butterflies and moths differ from other insects in their wings and mouthparts.

KEY
1 Wings
2 Thorax
3 Abdomen
4 Head
5 Eyes
6 Antennae
7 Legs

▶ A lepidopteran's wings and legs are all attached to its thorax.

LEPIDOPTERA
Butterflies and moths

MOTHS
Over 100 families.
Selected examples:

◀ This family tree shows some of the groups and subgroups of lepidopterans.

Bombycoidea
Silk, emperor, oon, sphinx and hawk moths

Noctuoidea
Noctuid or owlet moths, and tiger, underwing, snout, prominent and tuft moths

Tortricoidea
Tortrix, codling, leaf-roller and budworm moths

Geometroidea
Geometer (loopers and inchworms), and sunset moths

Pyraloidea
Snout, grass, meal, rice, flour and corn borer moths

4 The name Lepidoptera means 'scale wings'. It comes from the tiny scales on the wings and parts of the body and head. Most are about 0.1–0.2 mm long. There can be as many as 600 scales per sq mm of wing surface. They can be shaped like flaps, leaves or hairs, each overlapping and attached to the wing by a thin stem.

◀▲ A close-up of the Spanish moon moth's wing reveals the tiny different-coloured scales.

5 The scales have different shapes and colours, so light bounces off them in various ways. These effects can combine to make the wings look iridescent – colours such as purple shine through, but only when viewed at a certain angle.

6 Since ancient times, the beauty of butterflies and moths has fascinated people. Drawings and paintings of them, and the actual insects themselves, were used as decorations in many places, from caves to great temples, and on ornaments, brooches, clothes and head-dresses.

Moth or butterfly?

Love the light

In the hot African sun, small striped swordtail butterflies flock to sip mineral-rich water at the edge of a drying waterhole.

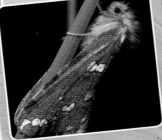

Fly-by-night

The gold swift moth of Europe is beautifully camouflaged to hide among old leaves, twigs and stems by day. It then emerges at dusk.

Day-flier

The Asian butterfly hawk moth is strong and fast. It flies speedily by day, searching for food and mates.

▲ Most moths are night-active, but not all.

7 There are several main differences between butterflies and moths. However, there are exceptions to all of them. For example, most butterflies are active by day, or diurnal, while moths tend to fly at night – nocturnal. Yet some moths, like the butterfly hawk moth, are day-fliers.

8 Butterflies generally have colourful wings and slender bodies. Many moths are brown, grey or similar dull colours, and have stout bodies. But there are many brilliantly colourful moths, especially in warm parts of the world.

▼ When resting, most moths hold their wings out flat, while butterflies fold them together over the back.

Bright and slender

The thin-bodied malachite butterfly, found in parts of the Americas, is named after the green mineral malachite.

Furry emperor

The Ligurnian emperor moth of central Europe has a hairy thorax and abdomen, and false 'eyes' on its wings.

Colourful creature

The day-flying false tiger moth of southern and southeast Asia has brilliant colours to warn predators it has a foul taste.

Alert antennae

In northwest North America, Taylor's checkerspot butterfly uses its wide-ended antennae to detect flower scents.

Feathery feelers

The male Japanese luna moth spreads his plume-like antennae to catch the pheromones (special scents) released by females of his species.

◄▲ All butterflies have club-ended antennae; very few moths do.

Club-ended

Australia's golden sun moth, one of the few species with clubbed antennae, is critically endangered in its specialized grassland habitat.

KEY
- ● Butterflies
- ● Moths
- ● Exceptions

9 Most butterflies have slim antennae with a wider part at the end, known as club-ended. Many moths have antennae that taper to a point, and in the males are frilly or feathery. But the castiniid moth family have club-ended antennae.

10 When a butterfly caterpillar enters the next stage of its life, it changes into a hard-cased pupa, or chrysalis. Many moth caterpillars also make an extra covering of silky threads, called a cocoon. Unusually, apollo butterflies spin cocoons like moths.

▼► Only a few butterfly caterpillars spin cocoons.

Soft touch

The ruby tiger moth of Europe and north Asia wraps itself in a cocoon of strong threads as it develops, or metamorphoses, into an adult.

11 Most moths have a tiny rod or spine, called a frenulum, near the body at the front of each rear wing. This fits into a hook known as the retinaculum, at the base of the front wing. This pairing makes the two wings on each side move together more effectively. Very few butterflies have this feature.

Hard cases

Found in southeast Asia, pupae of the large tree nymph butterfly are well-known for their shiny golden cases.

Silken cocoon

The clouded apollo butterfly of north Asia and Europe spins a cocoon of silken threads on the ground.

A closer look

12 Like other insects, butterflies and moths have a hard outer body covering called an exoskeleton. This is made of a tough substance called chitin. The exoskeleton covers nearly all of the body, even the legs and antennae, and gives strength and protection to the soft parts inside.

▼ This cutaway diagram shows the inner parts of the female golden birdwing butterfly.

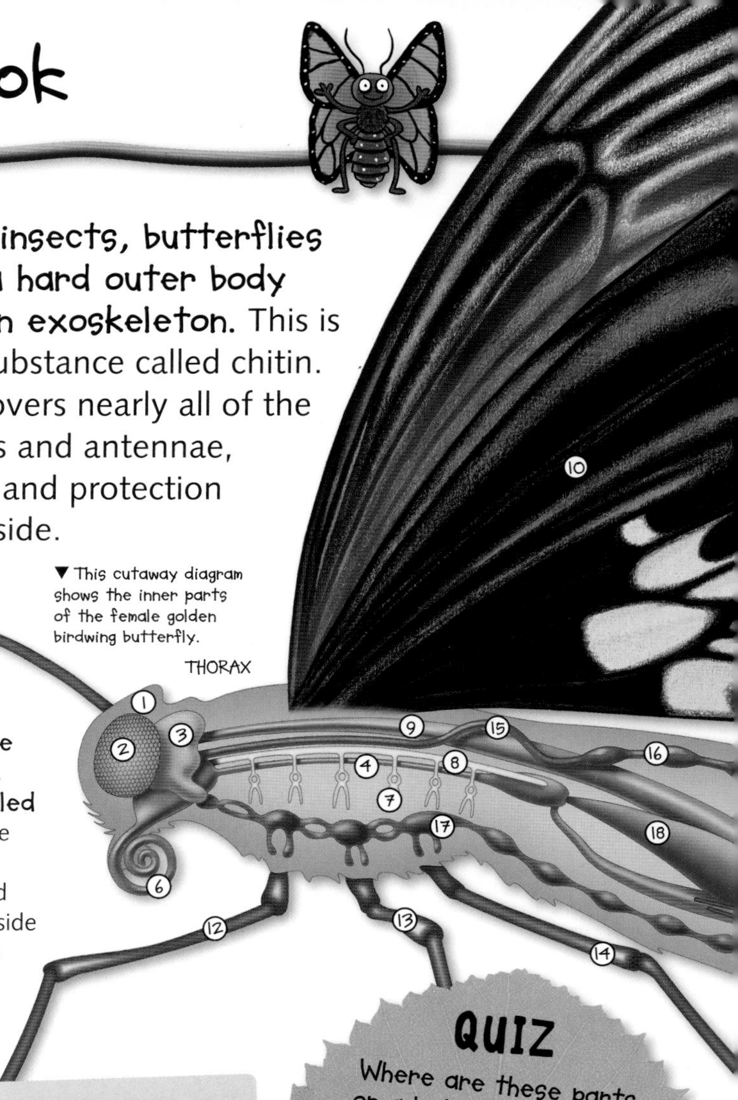

THORAX

13 The head has the mouthparts for feeding, including a long tube called the proboscis. Also on the head are the main sense organs such as the eyes and antennae (see page 14). Inside is the tiny brain, as small as the dot on this 'i'.

KEY

① Head	⑧ Lateral trachea	⑮ Main blood vessel
② Eye	⑨ Main dorsal trachea	⑯ Hearts
③ Brain	⑩ Fore (front) wing	⑰ Main nerve
④ Oesophagus	⑪ Hind (rear) wing	⑱ Crop (stomach)
⑤ Antenna	⑫ Fore (front) leg	⑲ Gut (intestines)
⑥ Proboscis	⑬ Middle leg	⑳ Excretory system
⑦ Spiracles	⑭ Hind (rear) leg	㉑ Reproductive parts

(see page 14)

QUIZ
Where are these parts on a butterfly or moth?
1. Waste removal system
2. Eyes
3. Wing-moving muscles
4. Veins

Answers:
1. Abdomen 2. Head
3. Thorax 4. Wings

14 Behind the head, the thorax is like a stiff, strong box. The wings and legs are attached to it by flexible joints. Inside it are powerful muscles that move the wings and legs. Through it passes the feeding tube, or oesophagus.

15 The fore or front wings, and the hind or rear wings, are wide, flat and thin. They are strengthened by tube-like structures called veins, which contain air tubes and a blood-like fluid, haemolymph. The fore wings are usually larger and more pointed, making them move through the air more easily.

ABDOMEN

▶ The wing veins of this common emigrant butterfly have a branching pattern.

16 Like other insects, butterflies and moths have three pairs of legs. Each is covered in scales and has about nine tube-like sections, ending in a foot with tiny claws or brush-like hairs.

▶ This geometer moth foot has tiny scales, two gripping claws and touch-sensitive hairs.

17 The abdomen contains the main digestive parts (crop and intestines), the excretory (waste-removal) system, and the reproductive parts. Like most of the body it has small air holes called spiracles. These lead to a network of tubes called the trachea that are the breathing system, passing air to all body parts.

Super senses

18 **Butterflies and moths have two antenna, or feelers.** Their tiny sensors detect substances they touch and also those in the air – such as pheromones released at breeding time (see page 18). Antennae also respond to heat, cold, and moving air or wind.

There are long, thin muscles inside the antenna, allowing it to bend

▼ Each eye has thousands of individual parts, forming a dome shape. This allows the butterfly or moth to detect movement over a wide area.

19 **A butterfly or moth eye is compound, made up of many tiny lenses called ommatidia.** Each detects a small area of the insect's view, and these many areas are combined by the brain into one large image, like a mosaic. The eyes can see certain colours and also ultraviolet light (which human eyes cannot detect). Some flowers have patterns that only show up in ultraviolet light, guiding the moth or butterfly to the nectar that it feeds on.

▶ Invisible in normal light (left), the marsh marigold's nectar guide patterns show up in ultraviolet light (right).

In normal light

Nerve to brain

Light-sensitive cells

Pigment (coloured) cells

Rhabdom (central rod)

Crystalline cone of lens

Cornea of lens

◀ Each ommatidium lets in light through a lens at the wide end.

20 Butterflies and moths can 'hear' with their antennae. They can also 'hear' with thin, bendy patches on the body surface that vibrate when hit by sound waves. These are called tympanal organs, and are usually on the thorax.

21 Some moths have 'ears' or tympanal organs on different parts of their bodies. Geometer moths have theirs at the front of the abdomen. Noctuid moths have them on the wings, to sense the clicks and squeaks of bats who hunt them at night.

22 Tiny organs allow butterflies and moths to both 'smell' and 'taste' with their feet. Known as olfactory organs, they respond to certain substances floating in the air (smell) and on surfaces (taste). So a butterfly or moth can tell as soon as it lands if a place is likely to have food or be harmful.

▶ Olfactory or smell organs are on various parts of this Chinese peacock butterfly, including its antennae and feet.

In ultraviolet light

15

Food and feeding

23 Most adult butterflies and moths have a long, tube-like mouthpart, the proboscis. Hardly any other insect has this. The proboscis is usually coiled up in a spiral under the head. To feed, it unrolls and works like a straw to suck up liquid foods or small food particles.

24 The main food of butterflies and moths is nectar, a sugary liquid that comes from flowers. They find nectar using their antennae, eyes, and smell and taste sensors on their feet. Another food is pollen grains, tiny particles made by male flower parts, which join with female parts to develop seeds and fruits.

Coiled up proboscis

▲ The coiled proboscis tucks out of the way under the head.

◄ The uncoiled proboscis can be longer than the whole body, as in Morgan's sphinx moth.

25 Insects that carry pollen are vital for flowers to reproduce. Butterflies and moths are second only to bees and wasps in helping this process. Certain flowers open only at the time of day or night, or year, when the butterflies and moths that feed on them are on the wing (active).

▲ Buddleia is known as the 'butterfly bush', as its nectar-rich flowers attract many species, such as these small tortoiseshell butterflies.

▼ Some pools attract large numbers of butterflies, like these orange sulphurs.

▼ A black king butterfly straightens its proboscis to sip from a puddle.

26 Some butterflies and moths feed on more unusual liquids. These include rotting fruit juices, and animal sweat, tears, urine or dung. Others gather at waterholes or muddy pools and 'puddle' – suck up the water to obtain nutrients. However, some have no working mouthparts and so do not feed at all.

27 Adult butterflies and moths rarely cause problems with their feeding. But a few species of caterpillars can be huge pests to people, causing damage worth millions of pounds. Different kinds eat farm crops, fruits, vegetables, garden flowers, tree buds and blossom, stored grains and other foods – even our clothes. The clothes moth caterpillar feeds on fabrics made of wool and other natural fibres.

Getting together

28 To breed or reproduce – make more of their kind – a female and male of the same species get together to mate. In many butterflies, the female and male look different – this is called sexual dimorphism. For example, the male adonis blue is bright blue in colour, while the female is dull blue-grey. The male vapourer moth has red-brown wings, but the female has tiny wings and cannot even fly.

▼ The male (below) and female (left) adonis blue butterflies almost look like different species.

29 In many moths, the female gives off special scents called pheromones from her abdomen. A male of her kind can detect it with his wide feathery antennae, perhaps from a kilometre or more away. The male of one of the largest moths, the atlas moth, has extra-large feathery antennae. Some males also make pheromones.

QUIZ

1. What colour is the female adonis blue butterfly?
2. What is the name of the special scents given off by females?
3. Why do males and females make courtship movements?

Answers:
1. Dull blue-grey 2. Pheromones 3. To check that the other is a suitable partner

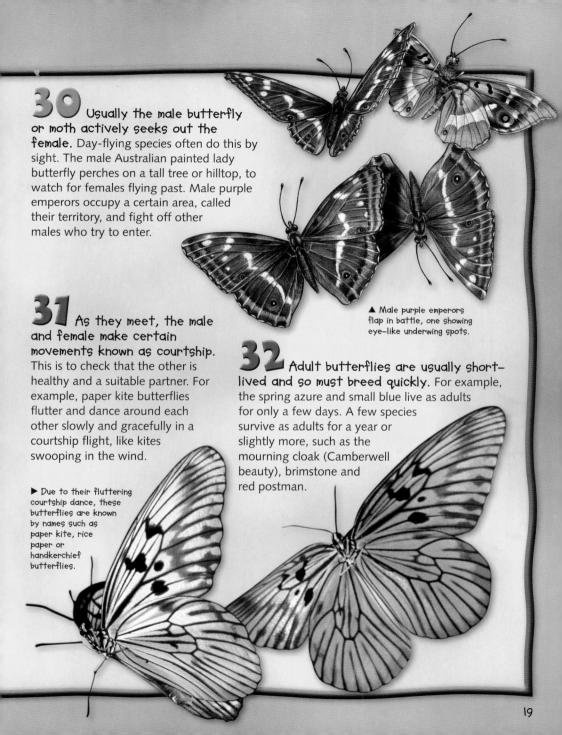

30 Usually the male butterfly or moth actively seeks out the female. Day-flying species often do this by sight. The male Australian painted lady butterfly perches on a tall tree or hilltop, to watch for females flying past. Male purple emperors occupy a certain area, called their territory, and fight off other males who try to enter.

▲ Male purple emperors flap in battle, one showing eye-like underwing spots.

31 As they meet, the male and female make certain movements known as courtship. This is to check that the other is healthy and a suitable partner. For example, paper kite butterflies flutter and dance around each other slowly and gracefully in a courtship flight, like kites swooping in the wind.

▶ Due to their fluttering courtship dance, these butterflies are known by names such as paper kite, rice paper or handkerchief butterflies.

32 Adult butterflies are usually short-lived and so must breed quickly. For example, the spring azure and small blue live as adults for only a few days. A few species survive as adults for a year or slightly more, such as the mourning cloak (Camberwell beauty), brimstone and red postman.

Growing up

33 **Butterflies and moths grow up in a series of stages, known as the life cycle.** During these stages – egg, caterpillar, chrysalis and adult – they change their shape greatly. This process is called metamorphosis. The adult female usually lays eggs on or near the plants the caterpillars will eat when they hatch. Ghost moths may lay over 10,000 eggs in one go.

34 **The eggs hatch into caterpillars, or larvae.** They start to eat at once. Few other animals have such huge appetites for their size. Most species have particular food plants, for example, small tortoiseshell, red admiral and peacock butterfly caterpillars all eat stinging nettles.

35 **The caterpillar's exoskeleton cannot stretch much.** So after a time it splits, the caterpillar wiggles out, enlarges and forms a new, bigger casing. This is known as shedding, moulting or ecdysis. Most caterpillars do this five times. Each stage is called an instar.

1 The female swallowtail butterfly lays its eggs on milk parsley, wild carrot, wild angelica, fennel, hogweed or clover. Only one egg is laid at a time

2 This first instar (stage) caterpillar is three days old and as small as a rice grain

▶ Selected stages from the life cycle of the Old World or common swallowtail butterfly.

3 By the third instar the caterpillar (larva) has grown hundreds of times bigger

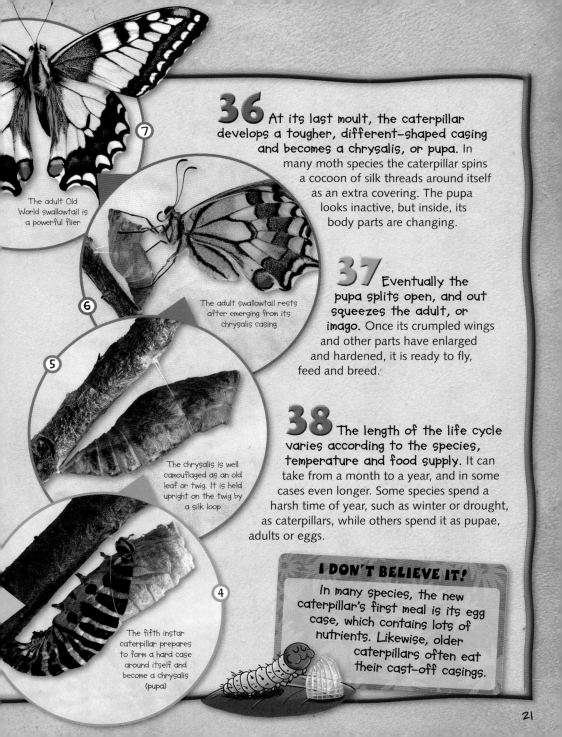

36 At its last moult, the caterpillar develops a tougher, different-shaped casing and becomes a chrysalis, or pupa. In many moth species the caterpillar spins a cocoon of silk threads around itself as an extra covering. The pupa looks inactive, but inside, its body parts are changing.

37 Eventually the pupa splits open, and out squeezes the adult, or imago. Once its crumpled wings and other parts have enlarged and hardened, it is ready to fly, feed and breed.

38 The length of the life cycle varies according to the species, temperature and food supply. It can take from a month to a year, and in some cases even longer. Some species spend a harsh time of year, such as winter or drought, as caterpillars, while others spend it as pupae, adults or eggs.

⑦

The adult Old World swallowtail is a powerful flier

⑥

The adult swallowtail rests after emerging from its chrysalis casing

⑤

The chrysalis is well camouflaged as an old leaf or twig. It is held upright on the twig by a silk loop

④

The fifth instar caterpillar prepares to form a hard case around itself and become a chrysalis (pupa)

I DON'T BELIEVE IT!

In many species, the new caterpillar's first meal is its egg case, which contains lots of nutrients. Likewise, older caterpillars often eat their cast-off casings.

Clever caterpillars

39 Caterpillars look very different from adult butterflies and moths. They lack wings, and the head, thorax and abdomen are difficult to tell apart. They have small eyes and feelers shaped like teeth, called palps, to taste food. Instead of a proboscis, caterpillars have scissor-like mouthparts called mandibles, to cut and chew food.

▶ A caterpillar's 'jaws' or mandibles work with a side-to-side motion, like hook-shaped scissors.

Mandible

Palp

40 A caterpillar has three pairs of legs on the thorax, like an adult, although these are much shorter. It also has up to five extra pairs of stumpy legs on the abdomen, known as prolegs. The caterpillar crawls by moving these legs forwards and backwards, and also makes its body longer and shorter by arching up and down.

◀ 'Looper' caterpillars arch the front of the body up, extend forwards and down, then pull the rear along too.

Prolegs

41 Caterpillars are vital parts of nature's food chains. They are soft and slow, and so can be easy prey for predators such as shrews, rats, birds, lizards, frogs and praying mantises. Millions of caterpillars are eaten every year.

42 However, many caterpillars can defend themselves. Some taste horrible, due to substances they get from their food. They often have bright markings in 'warning colours' such as red, yellow and black. Predators will remember the bad taste and avoid similar colours in future.

43 Some caterpillars have a coat of long hairs to protect themselves. These break easily to release a fluid that stings or irritates the predator. Such caterpillars are often known as 'woolly bears'.

▶ The garden tiger moth's 'woolly bear' caterpillar has long hairs, setae, that cause redness and irritation when touched.

44 Another method of defence is for a caterpillar to rear up and look fierce. In doing this, some display bright eye-like patterns, wave a long 'horn' or squirt foul liquid. The puss moth caterpillar has a bendy red section on each of its tails that flick to frighten predators.

◀ The puss moth caterpillar displays its red front and flips its long tail whips at enemies.

Families of moths

45 Animals that are closely related and similar to each other are organized into groups called families. There are more than 100 main families of moths. Some consist of thousands of species, others far fewer. The Opostegidae family, known as white eyecap moths, has fewer than 200 species.

Geometrid family

▲ This geometrid 'looper' caterpillar is coloured to resemble a small twig.

46 The largest moth family is the noctuids or owlet moths. It has more than 35,000 species – about one in five of all moths. The owlet, underwing, dagger, forester, dart and silver-Y moths all belong to this group. Most are dull-coloured, but the burnished brass moth has bright metallic patches on its upper wings.

▶ The burnished brass moth has shiny green patches like old brass.

47 Another very large family is the geometrids or geometer moths, with about 26,000 species. It includes wave, mocha and emerald moths. Their caterpillars are known as loopers, spanworms or inchworms from the way they arch their bodies into an upside-down U or loop as they move along.

Noctuid family

48 The saturnid family includes royal, emperor, atlas and giant moths, with around 2000 species. They are among the biggest of all moths, and of all lepidopterans – even of all insects. The regal moth of North America has greyish wings 15 centimetres across, with brown stripes and pale spots.

Saturnid family

▶ The adult regal moth has no working mouthparts and only lives for about a week.

Sphingid family

49 Hawk moths and sphinx moths belong to the sphingid family. It has about 1500 species. Sphingids have large bodies and sweptback wings that beat very rapidly, making them speedy fliers. Some hawk moths can even hover in mid-air, like flies and hummingbirds.

◀ The bee hawk moth hovers near a flower, preparing to feed.

Butterfly families

50 Like moths, closely related butterflies are grouped into families. The largest is the nymphalids, with over 6000 species such as emperors, monarchs, admirals and fritillaries. In most, the front legs are unusually small with brush-like ends, giving them the name brush-footed butterflies. The upper wing surfaces are brightly coloured.

Nymphalid family

▲ The great purple emperor, a nymphalid, is patterned above but its underwings are plain.

51 The lycaenid family is the second biggest. It has more than 5000 species of blues, coppers, hairstreaks, elfins, harvesters and woolly-legs. They are generally small and shiny. In certain species their caterpillars feed on insects such as aphids and ants.

▼ A slug-like lycaenid moth-butterfly caterpillar preys on ant larvae.

52 The hesperiids, or skippers, are named after their fast darting or 'skipping' flight. Skippers are often classified separately from butterflies. They have moth-like features such as a tubby body and relatively small wings, and antennae with hooked or bent ends, rather than clubbed.

Lycaenid family

Papilionid family

53 Swallowtails, birdwings and apollos are in the papilionid family. Most of the 550 species are big and brightly coloured, with trailing flaps, tails or strips on the rear wings that resemble the deep-forked tail of the swallow bird.

▼ A common rose swallowtail shows its streamer-like rear wing 'tails'.

▼ Hedylids are classed as butterflies but have many moth-like features, such as drab colours.

Hedylid family

54 The pierid family contains some 1100 species of whites, yellows, sulphurs, orange-tips and oranges. Some have dark spots and patches. Another small family, with 1500 species, is the shiny-winged riodinids. They include harlequin and punch butterflies. The smallest is the moth-like hedylids or American moth-butterflies, with 35 species.

▼ Riodinids such as the common red harlequin are known as metalmarks due to their shiny patches.

MAKE A NEW SPECIES

You will need:
thin card scissors glue
shiny coloured paper, foil, sweet wrappers, etc.

Draw and cut out a big butterfly shape using the card. Cut out shiny coloured circles, diamonds, stripes and other shapes and glue them onto the wings. Think of a name for your new species, make a label and put it on display.

Riodinid family

Cunning camouflage

55 Few creatures have such amazing camouflage as adult butterflies and moths. They often look like common objects found in nature that are not tasty or edible, so predators leave them alone. Hunters of butterflies and moths include many birds that can see well in colour, which is why camouflage is so important.

56 Many moths are inactive by day and are camouflaged as twigs, dead leaves, bark and stones. Peppered moths exactly match the lichen-covered tree trunks where they rest. Some butterflies close their wings to hide the bright upper surfaces. The lower surfaces can look like leaves, either fresh and green, or brown and dead.

LIGHT AND DARK
Most peppered moths have pale and dark speckles (right) for camouflage on lichen-covered trees. Darker or melanic forms (left) regularly occur but they are easily seen and caught by predators.

During the Industrial Revolution, trees became covered in soot. The melanic form was better camouflaged and so became more common. Less pollution in modern times means the original form is again becoming more common.

► The Kallima dead-leaf butterfly bears an astonishing resemblance to an old brown leaf, even down to the veins.

▲ This giant swallowtail butterfly caterpillar has the shiny, damp appearance of fresh bird droppings.

57 It is not only adults that have camouflage. Many caterpillars have green and brown patterns to match the leaves and twigs of their food plants. Some even resemble animal droppings that predators ignore, such as the caterpillar of the giant swallowtail butterfly, which looks like bird droppings.

58 Pupae are also often well camouflaged. This is because they cannot move while the caterpillar inside changes into an adult, and so are vulnerable to predators. Again, common kinds of camouflage include twigs, leaves and bark, often hidden among bushes and trees. The common mime butterfly, found in Asia, has a pupa that looks just like a twig attached to a stem — even down to its broken end.

▶ The common mime pupa looks like a broken twig, with brown streaks and a snapped-off end.

▶ Several kinds of butterfly pupae, such as this emerald swallowtail, are bright green and so 'disappear' among fresh leaves.

Survival tricks

59 **Butterflies and moths use trickery, deceit and pretence to survive.** Some have large rounded eye-like patterns, eyespots, on their wings. These are usually hidden, but the butterfly or moth can suddenly move its wings to display them. They look like the eyes of a cat, hawk, owl or similar fierce creature, and so can frighten away predators.

Eyespot

▲ The Io moth's front wings move aside to reveal glaring predator-like 'eyes' on its rear wings.

60 **Like caterpillars, some adults have bright warning colours and patterns, such as yellow and black, or red and black.** These tell predators that they taste horrible or are poisonous. After a predator has tried to eat one, it recognizes the warning colours and avoids others with those colours.

61 **Different distasteful species sometimes have very similar warning colours.** After a predator encounters one of them, it avoids any similar-coloured creatures. This kind of similarity is known as Mullerian mimicry.

▼ Tiger-striped, tiger and numata longwing butterflies share similar colours to show they taste horrible.

Tiger-striped longwing

Tiger longwing

Numata longwing

◀ The pipevine swallowtail's flesh tastes foul, yet its mimic...

◀ ...the spicebush swallowtail, which looks so similar, is tasty to predators.

62 Other species have warning colours – yet they are quite tasty! This kind of pretence is called Batesian mimicry. The pretender, or mimic, looks similar to a distasteful or poisonous species, so predators tend to avoid the mimic as well.

63 In other forms of mimicry, butterflies and moths pretend to be very different kinds of animals. They mimic creatures that their predators do not usually eat, such as wasps and spiders, and even toads and snakes. The atlas moth's front wingtip resembles a snake's head, complete with eye and mouth slit.

◀ The Atlas moth's snake-head wing pattern.

64 There can also be different colour forms of the same species. Known as polymorphs, these breed together as usual, but they look quite unlike each other. Each form, or morph, may mimic another, different species. So for a predator, knowing which species is which, and whether it tastes good or bad, is difficult.

QUIZ

1. Which colours are examples of warning colours?
2. Which animal does the atlas moth's front wingtip resemble?
3. What is the name for different colour forms of the same species?

Answers:
1. Yellow and black, and red and black 2. A snake 3. Polymorphs

31

On the wing

65 Nearly all kinds of butterflies and moths can fly as adults. They fly to avoid predators, find food, locate mates, and in some species, travel to places with better conditions. Despite their delicate appearance, they are powerful fliers. However, some female moths have tiny wings or none at all, such as the winter moth.

66 Butterfly and moth wings beat in a similar way to those of some other insects. They are hinged onto the thorax, which is like a stiff box. Two sets of muscles inside the thorax make it alternately lower, then higher, causing the wings to flick up and down.

Vertical muscles pull so top of thorax bends down

Wings flip up

Wings flip down

Horizontal muscles pull so top of thorax bends up

▲ The thorax works like a stiff-walled box, flipping the wings up and down.

▼ In general, larger species of butterflies and moths flap their wings more slowly than smaller ones.

How fast do they flap?

Atlas moths
Number of wingbeats per second: **5–10**

White butterflies
Number of wingbeats per second: **12**

Skipper butterflies
Number of wingbeats per second: **20**

Cutworm moths
Number of wingbeats per second: **30–60**

Leaf-miner moths
Number of wingbeats per second: **over 200**

67 Although most remain in a small area, some species take to the air in mass flights for long-distance migrations. The monarch butterfly is famous for this (see next page). Every year in Australia, millions of bogong moths migrate from the plains of New South Wales and Queensland, to spend summer in the cooler Snowy Mountains to the south. Attracted by the lights, they land in huge numbers in cities such as Canberra and Sydney.

▲ Migrating bogong moths can cause chaos in cities, getting into buildings and vehicles and clogging up air conditioning.

▲ The two wings on either side change angle as they flap together, as on this cecropia moth.

68 Certain butterflies and moths undergo irruptions. This is when good conditions every few years, such as calm weather and plenty of food, mean there's a huge increase in numbers. They then fly off in swarms to find new places to feed and breed. This happens occasionally to underwing moths in parts of Europe.

the greatest traveller

69 Of all butterflies and moths, the North American monarch or milkweed butterfly is the greatest traveller. In winter, adults roost (rest) on trees in California, Florida and other southern states, as well as Mexico – all places with mild winters. At some roosts, many thousands of adults cluster together.

◄ Trees at monarch roosting sites can be completely covered with butterflies jostling for space and the sun's warmth.

I DON'T BELIEVE IT!
In 2009 monarch caterpillars were taken to the International Space Station. They became pupae and then adults onboard, fluttering in the weightless environment.

70 In spring the adults fly north and northeast. After a time they pause to breed, laying eggs that hatch after 3 to 8 days. The caterpillars eat milkweeds and similar plants that contain distasteful substances, which make them taste awful – as shown by their warning colours of yellow, white and black.

► Monarch caterpillars grow fast, reaching almost 5 centimetres in length.

► The pupa hangs from a twig by a silk thread.

① Fat, mature monarch caterpillars pupate. During this time of metamorphosis their bodies develop into adults.

② Body parts, such as the wings and abdomen, are visible on the pupa.

③ An adult monarch emerges. Its body is still soft and will have to harden before the butterfly can take flight and continue its migration.

71 After moulting five times over 9 to 16 days, the caterpillars become green pupae. After another 9 to 15 days the adults emerge, continue their northward migration, then stop and breed to produce another generation. This can happen three or four times in the same migration, as adult monarchs only live for 2 to 6 weeks. Some monarchs reach as far north as Canada, 4000 kilometres from the winter roosts.

CANADA

USA

MEXICO

72 Towards the end of summer, the final generation of adults make one non-stop flight back to the roost sites. In doing this, they avoid the harsh northern winter. This is the longest journey of any insect, and even of most creatures. After a winter rest, the whole cycle begins again.

◄ This map shows the main migration routes of monarchs across North America.

73 Such long-distance migrations may have begun long ago when the butterflies' roost sites were close to their feeding areas. Over time, climate and other changes separated these areas, and the butterflies gradually developed greater power and strength in flight.

We are the champions

74 **Butterflies and moths are some of the largest insects.** The species with the greatest wingspan is the white witch moth of Central and South America, at 30 centimetres or more. The Hercules moth of Southeast Asia and Australia, and the Atlas moth also of Southeast Asia, have wingspans of about 28 centimetres. However, they have the largest wing area, up to 400 square centimetres.

▶ The white witch moth is also called the giant ghost moth.

Heaviest

75 **The giant carpenter moth of Australia is the heaviest adult butterfly or moth.** It weighs up to 20 grams. But it is only half as heavy as the Atlas moth caterpillar, which can weigh over 50 grams.

▲ Atlas moth caterpillars weigh twice as much as the adult moths.

Smallest

76 **Tiniest butterflies include the Western pygmy blue of North America, with a wingspan of 1.5 centimetres.** Far smaller are pygmy leaf-miner moths of the Nepticulidae family. Living in many regions but especially Australia and southern Asia, the feather-like wings of some species measure just 3 millimetres across.

▶ The white area of this bramble leaf shows where a golden pygmy moth caterpillar has eaten through it. The caterpillar grew as it ate.

77 The hungriest caterpillars are those of the polyphemus moth of North America. In less than two months they eat more than 60,000 times their own weight in leafy food – that's about the same as a person eating five million lettuces.

HANGING MOBILE

You will need:
thin card   colouring pencils
scissors   chopsticks, dowels or
similar   thin string

Find some pictures of the record-holding butterflies and moths featured on these pages. Draw them life-size on card, cut them out and colour them in. Attach them to the chopsticks or dowels with string to make a hanging mobile – which will need plenty of room!

78 The Arctic woolly bear moth has the longest life cycle – it takes seven years to develop from egg to adult. Almost all of this is spent in the hairy 'woolly bear' caterpillar stage. Due to chemicals produced in its body, the caterpillar can stand being frozen solid for up to 11 months each year, thawing out to feed for a few weeks, then freezing again. This happens around seven times before the caterpillar is ready to pupate.

Longest life cycle

▼ The Arctic caterpillar has natural 'anti-freeze' substances in its blood. When temperatures start to drop, it spins a protective cocoon in which it stays until it thaws out.

Evolution long ago

79 **Like all animals, butterflies and moths have developed over time.** We know this from their fossils – remains preserved in rock. The first moth fossils date back to the time of the early dinosaurs – the Jurassic Period, almost 200 million years ago. One of the earliest was *Archaeolepis*, a moth with a wingspan of about one centimetre. Its wing scales and other features were similar to the moth and butterfly cousins, caddisflies.

80 **Moth fossils become more varied from the start of the Cretaceous Period, around 145 million years ago.** This was also when the first flowers evolved. As new kinds of flowers developed, new species of lepidopterans evolved to feed on them, such as tiger moths.

◄ Magnolias were among the first flowers to appear.

81 **One of the earliest butterflies was the beautifully patterned *Prodryas*.** It was fossilized about 40 million years ago during the Paleogene Period. With wings 1–2 centimetres long, it was a relative of today's mapwing and admiral butterflies, in the nymphalid family.

▼ *Prodryas*, with a wingspan of 2.5 centimetres, resembled today's mapwings, like the little map shown here.

I DON'T BELIEVE IT!

Tiny preserved moth wing scales have been found in the stomachs of fossilized lizards from over 100 million years ago!

◄ Baltic amber from 40 million years ago has preserved all parts of this moth – even the contents of its gut.

82 Butterflies and moths have been perfectly preserved by being trapped in amber. This is the yellow or gold-coloured fluid known as resin that oozes from certain trees and then hardens. Amber from the Baltic region in Europe shows many kinds of butterflies and moths from 50–40 million years ago.

Habitats galore

83 Butterflies and moths, like most kinds of living things, thrive best in warm, damp climates. The tropical rainforest habitats around the middle of the Earth are hot or warm all year, with plenty of moisture that encourages plants and flowers. There are more kinds of butterflies and moths here than in all other habitats combined.

▼ Several kinds of blue morpho butterflies live in Central and South America.

Owl butterfly
Habitat: Dense lowland rainforest
Range: Southern North America to northern South America

Dirce beauty butterfly
Habitat: Open rainforest, shrubland
Range: Central and northern South America

Postman butterfly
Habitat: Open forest, scattered woodland
Range: Central America to southern Brazil

84 To attract mates, tropical butterflies and moths often have brilliant patterns. These help them stand out even among the bright flowers and other colourful creatures. One of the shiniest is the blue morpho butterfly, with bright blue wings that catch the light. The wings of the harmonia mantle butterfly contain almost every colour of the rainbow.

QUIZ
1. In what type of climates do butterflies and moths thrive?
2. How do species in tropical rainforests attract mates?
3. Why are tropical grassland species powerful fliers?

Answers:
1. Warm and damp
2. They have brilliant patterns
3. They search for flowers among the grasses

▲ The tropics extend either side of the Equator around the middle of the Earth, and harbour the world's richest wildlife.

▲ Tropical wetlands provide many places for 'puddling' – including the head of this caiman, a type of crocodile.

85 Tropical wetlands such as mangrove swamps are home to thousands of species. Many kinds, such as the Sunderbans crow butterfly, breed when water levels are low, and plants grow well. When the rainy season brings floods, they migrate to drier areas.

86 Species that live in tropical grasslands are generally powerful fliers as they have to search for flowers among the grasses. With a wingspan of 2 centimetres, the male African wild silkmoth is half the size of the female and flies more swiftly. People collect the threads from its cocoons and make them into silken fabrics.

Rajah Brooke's birdwing butterfly
Habitat: Thick rainforest
Range: Southeast Asia

Comet moth
Habitat: Dense to open rainforest
Range: Madagascar

▼ Just one silkmoth cocoon can produce a thread of raw silk up to one kilometre long.

87 Another kind of moth that spins a silken cocoon is the mulberry silk moth. Its caterpillars, or 'silkworms', eat mulberry tree leaves. For thousands of years its cocoons have been used to make the finest silk fabrics – a business worth £300 million each year. However due to centuries of special breeding, these moths must spend their whole life cycle in captivity. In their natural habitat they would perish from heat, cold, predators and disease.

From mountains to cities

88 Temperate woodland is a rich habitat for butterflies and moths. These areas have a warm spring and summer, and cool autumn and winter. Various species' life cycles are timed to allow them to feed on leaves as caterpillars, and then on flowers as adults. Across Europe and Asia, the brimstone is one of the first butterflies on the wing each year. It spends the winter as an adult hibernating in vegetation, and may wake up on a warmer day even with snow still on the ground.

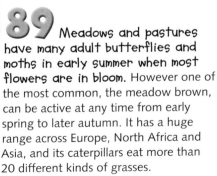

Woodland skipper
Habitat: Woods, shrubland, grassland,
Range: West to central North America

▼ The meadow brown butterfly lives among grasslands, fields, orchards, parks and gardens.

▶ There are temperate areas throughout the world, providing rich habitats for butterflies and moths.

89 Meadows and pastures have many adult butterflies and moths in early summer when most flowers are in bloom. However one of the most common, the meadow brown, can be active at any time from early spring to later autumn. It has a huge range across Europe, North Africa and Asia, and its caterpillars eat more than 20 different kinds of grasses.

◀ Buckthorn shrubs are the brimstone caterpillar's only food plant. The adult has a more varied diet.

Orange-tip butterfly
Habitat: Fields and other open areas
Range: Temperate Europe and Asia

White plume moth
Habitat: Mixed, from woods to gardens
Range: Europe

Six-spot burnet moth
Habitat: Meadows, cliffs, dunes, hedges, wood edges
Range: Europe, East Asia

Plain tiger butterfly
Habitat: Open country from hills to deserts
Range: Southern Europe to Southeast Asia

90 Heaths, moors and mountains are also home to a variety of butterfly and moth species. In North America the Rocky Mountain dotted blue butterfly depends mainly on buckwheat plants. The caterpillars eat the leaves, then the adults drink nectar from the flowers. High in the European Alps, the mountain apollo butterfly flies powerfully for kilometres, even in strong winds, to find flowers with nectar.

▼ The mountain apollo butterfly ranges across Europe's uplands and mountains, from Spain to Central Asia.

91 Butterflies and moths are often found in urban habitats in towns and cities, especially in gardens where people plant nectar-rich flowers. The buddleia, which grows on wasteland in cities, is also called the 'butterfly bush' because it attracts so many species (see page 17). In South Africa the caterpillars of the garden acraea butterfly eat wild peach tree leaves and the adults visit passion flowers – both popular urban plants.

Pap. fusce Albo & Rubro maculati.

Pap. Cculati.

Englishman James Petiver (1665–1718) made one of the first butterfly collections.

Queen Alexandra's birdwing, the world's largest butterfly, is endangered due to collecting.

92 The scientific study of butterflies and moths began in 18th-century Europe. Its experts are known as lepidopterists. In the 19th century explorers travelled the world to catch specimens for collections and museums, making some species rare. It still occurs today, despite laws put in place to protect wildlife.

93 Habitat loss is a giant problem for many butterfly and moth species. Areas such as forests and wetlands are converted to houses, farms and factories. One of the first recorded extinctions caused by habitat loss was that of Sloane's urania moth of Jamaica. Already rare from collecting, it became extinct by 1910 as the island's lowland forests were cleared for timber and farmland.

The day-flying Sloane's urania moth was black with red, blue and green markings.

94 Also harmful are pesticide and herbicide chemicals, used to rid our food crops of pests and weeds. Caterpillars and adults are especially vulnerable when herbicides kill their food plants. Monarch butterflies have suffered due to loss of the milkweed plants they feed on. Non-chemical or biological control is a less damaging alternative. For example, parasites may be used to infest only the crop's pest species, leaving other plants and animals unharmed.

95 Climate change is a threat to much wildlife, including butterflies and moths. For example, plants flowering earlier due to higher temperatures may mean the blooms are not around when adult butterflies or moths need to feed on them. This leads to 'uncoupling' of food chains, which can upset the entire balance of nature.

Edith's checkerspot butterfly of western North America is becoming rarer due to climate change.

Invasive plants such as crown vetch can crowd out local butterfly or moth food plants.

96 Other threats include non-native or alien species being introduced. The introduced species may be plants that smother a lepidopteran's local food plant, or a new predator. There may be introduced parasites such as tiny wasps or flies whose grubs (larvae) eat any life stage, or diseases caused by bacteria, viruses and moulds.

Hopes for the future

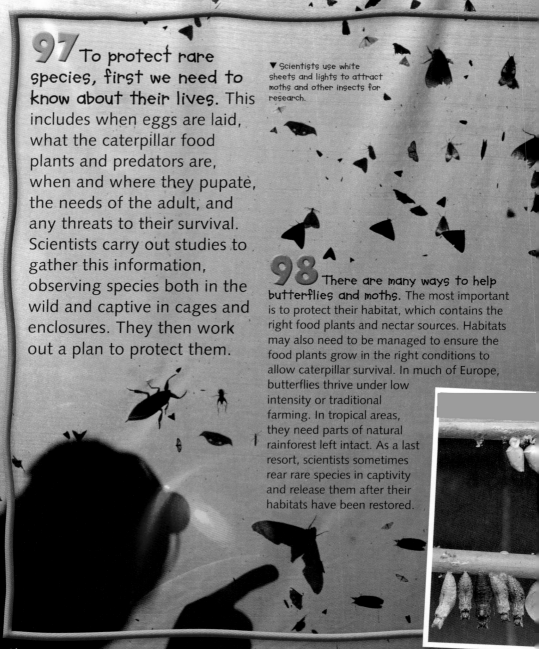

97 To protect rare species, first we need to know about their lives. This includes when eggs are laid, what the caterpillar food plants and predators are, when and where they pupate, the needs of the adult, and any threats to their survival. Scientists carry out studies to gather this information, observing species both in the wild and captive in cages and enclosures. They then work out a plan to protect them.

▼ Scientists use white sheets and lights to attract moths and other insects for research.

98 There are many ways to help butterflies and moths. The most important is to protect their habitat, which contains the right food plants and nectar sources. Habitats may also need to be managed to ensure the food plants grow in the right conditions to allow caterpillar survival. In much of Europe, butterflies thrive under low intensity or traditional farming. In tropical areas, they need parts of natural rainforest left intact. As a last resort, scientists sometimes rear rare species in captivity and release them after their habitats have been restored.

► Keen children learn how to use a butterfly net safely.

99 Education is also vital.

People can be informed about the fascinating lives of butterflies and moths, and their importance to pollination and food chains. Butterfly houses, nature reserves and watching events raise awareness and encourage people to get involved.

100 As individuals, we can all help butterflies and moths.

For example, it is easy to grow food plants for caterpillars and adults – anywhere from a windowbox to a large garden. Old leaves, log piles, weed patches and similar places are ideal for them to shelter during winter. Schools and clubs can also create butterfly gardens and similar projects. It all helps to conserve these beautiful, fascinating and vital creatures for the future.

MAKE A GARDEN

Find out about making a butterfly and moth garden. Packets of specially chosen 'butterfly mix' seeds can be sown in flowerpots, troughs, windowboxes or a corner of the garden, to provide food plants. Your local wildlife trust probably has a lepidopterist who can give advice.

◄ Captive breeding provides individuals to release into the wild.

Index

Page numbers in **bold** refer to main entries, those in *italics* refer to illustrations